OUR PORTRAIT IN GENESIS

Oswald Chambers' Publications—

OUR PORTRAIT
IN
GENESIS

OSWALD CHAMBERS

OSWALD CHAMBERS PUBLICATIONS
ASSOCIATION

and

MARSHALL, MORGAN & SCOTT
London

MARSHALL, MORGAN & SCOTT
BLUNDELL HOUSE
GOODWOOD ROAD
LONDON SE14 6BL

First published 1957
Second impression (paperback) 1972

ISBN 0 551 05157 4

PRINTED PHOTOLITHO IN GREAT BRITAIN BY
J. W. ARROWSMITH LTD., BRISTOL

FOREWORD

"Now these things were our examples" (1 *Corinthians* x. 6)

We know nothing of the beginning of life on this planet Earth unless we accept the revealed facts recorded in the Bible. When these early stories are accepted as a true record of individual lives we can learn much about God's dealings with men and women in every age. There are flashes of light on God's relation to fallen Man which can touch a live nerve in a modern wrong-doer, and something of the Divine mercy is seen as it persists with perverse and misguided men.

Oswald Chambers brings out the moral significance of human conduct; the intrusion of sin into human affairs, and God's counter-move against sin and against the Satanic power behind the scenes. "Now these things were our examples", wrote the Apostle Paul in reference to some Old Testament incidents. This can be applied to Cain and Abel, to Noah, and to Abraham ("in these things they became figures of us" —R.V. margin) as we see the subtle working of sin in the unregenerate human heart; of craftiness and insincerity between man and man; of the law of retribution on the one hand or the due recompense on the other.

Here is a book for to-day. The Spirit of God is revealing the deep things of God, especially as they bear on the deep things of humanity. Above all we hear of the God of all grace, Who gave His Son to be a propitiation for our sins—yours and mine—"and not for ours only, but also for the whole world."

I thank God for this gallery of portraits in Genesis, and for the Spirit's illumination through the expositor's instructed and clear-seeing mind.

David Lambert

CONTENTS

BEGINNINGS

Chapters i–ii

"In the beginning God" (ch. i. 1).

"I am Alpha and Omega, the beginning and the ending, saith the Lord, which is and which was, and which is to come, the Almighty" (Revelation i. 8).

The Bible never argues or debates, it states revelation facts, and in order to understand these facts we are dependent entirely, not on intellectual curiosity, but on a relationship of faith. Our perception of Bible truth is of the nature of implicit vision granted by the Holy Spirit, and the remarkable thing about the Holy Spirit's illumination of Bible truth is that it commends itself as being the true interpretation to every child of God who is in the light.

Science (knowledge systematized) is man's intellectual effort to expound established facts, facts which all intelligent men accept as facts; it is his attempt to arrange these facts into some kind of unity which will not contradict the fundamental way man is made. When we are born again we come in contact with another domain of facts, viz., the Bible domain of revelation facts, and there must be an at-one-ment made between the two domains. Scientific 'truth' is apt to be accepted readily while we are sceptical over revelations made by the Holy Spirit. Our tendency is to put truth into a dogma: Truth is a Person. *"I am the Truth"*, said Jesus.

"In the beginning God created the heaven and the earth.

And the earth was without form, and void" ("waste and void" R.V., ch. i. 1–2).

"Through faith we understand that the worlds were framed by the word of God, so that things which are seen were not made of things which do appear" (Hebrews xi. 3).

Fundamentally, chaos—the state of matter before it was reduced to order by the Creator—is not to be regarded necessarily as the result of Divine judgment but as the foundation of cosmos, like a painter's palette where he mixes his colours: he sees in it what you cannot. "Bairns and fools shouldn't see half-done work." We must bear in mind that the constructed world of man we see to-day is not the created world of God. The basis of man's life has had a formation put upon it which is not of God; what is needed is not the re-forming of the basis, but the removal of that which has been erected on the basis. If I build my life on the things which God did not form He will have to destroy them, shake them back into chaos. That is why whenever a man, moral or immoral, sees for the first time the light of God in Jesus Christ it produces conviction of sin, and he cries out, "Depart from me; for I am a sinful man, O Lord." When the Holy Spirit comes into a man 'his beauty is consumed away', the perfectly ordered completeness of his whole nature is broken up; then the Holy Spirit, brooding over the chaos that is produced, brings a word of God, and as that word is received and obeyed a new life is formed.

"And the spirit of God moved upon ("was brooding upon" R.V. marg.) the face of the waters. And God said, Let there be light: and there was light." God's word creates, and creates by its own power. God speaks, and His word performs that which He sends it to accomplish (cf. Isaiah lv. 11). "And God saw the light, that it was good:" The matter of God's creation

2

is a satisfaction to God, and when we come to know God by His Spirit we are as delighted with His creation as He is Himself. A child enjoys all that God has created, everything is wonderful to him.

As in the beginning God's word was the creative fiat, and that word's witness to itself satisfied God, so the work of Christ in a disciple witnesses to Him; it is the Living Word speaking the words, "the words that I speak unto you, they are spirit and they are life." My value to God is that in obedience to His spoken word I present to Him in actuality His idea in sending it forth, God's word expressed in me becomes its own witness to God. God's word is clear and emphatic, and when we first hear it we are full of joy; then that word has to become its own witness and give Him satisfaction. The fanatic mistakes the vision which the word brings for its expression in actuality. Am I prepared to put God's word into its right place, into the matter of 'me'? If I am, it will bring forth, not my idea, but God's idea, viz., the life according to God. It is not my faith laying hold of the word, but the life in the word laying hold on me and faith is as natural as breathing, and I say, 'Why, bless God, I *know* that is true!' Strictly speaking, no seed germ contains in itself the maturer growth, it is the other forces acting outside it as well as its own inherent life that determines what it will be ultimately.

"And God saw every thing that He had made, and behold, it was very good. And God blessed the seventh day, and hallowed it: because that in it He rested from all His work which God had created and made" (ch. i. 31; ii. 3).

Six days God laboured, *thinking* Creation, until, as He thought, so it was. On the seventh day God rested, not from fatigue, but because that work was finished which enabled Him to rest, immanent in all the laws of Nature, in constant manifestation of His overruling power, so that it were as easy for God to perform a miracle to-day as "in the beginning."

"And the Lord God formed man of the dust of the ground" (ch. ii 7).

"The first man is of the earth, earthy:" (1 Corinthians xv. 47).

These verses refer to the fundamental nature of man, don't complicate their meaning by introducing the doctrine of sin at the moment. These two things, dust and Divinity, make up man. That he is made of the dust of the ground is man's glory, not his shame—it is only his shame in so far as he is a sinner, because in it he is to manifest the image of God. We are apt to think because we are "of the earth, earthy," that this is our humiliation, but it is not so; it is the very thing God's word makes most of. A doctrine which has insinuated itself right into the heart of Christianity and has a hold on it like an octopus, is the inveterate belief that sin is in matter, therefore as long as there is any 'matter' about me there must be sin in me. If sin were in matter it would be untrue to say that Jesus Christ was "without sin" because He took on Him our flesh and blood, "becoming in the likeness of men". Sin does not belong to human nature as God designed it, it is abnormal, therefore to speak of sin being 'eradicated', rooted up, is nonsense, it never was planted in. I have no business to say, 'in Christ I am all right but in myself I am all wrong'; I have to see to it that everything related to my physical life is lived in harmony with and perfect obedience to the life of the Son of God in me.

The Originator and Maintainer of the new life

imparted to us by the Redemption is Christ Himself, and our Lord's words in John vi. 56 reveal His fathomless conception of that life—"he that eateth My flesh, and drinketh My blood, dwelleth in Me, and I in him." Before, the disposition of self-will ruled—You touch my flesh, and I hit you back; you touch my blood, and it boils in passion. Now, says Jesus, let the very corpuscles of your blood, every nerve and cell of your flesh, exhibit the new life which has been created in you. That life is exhibited in this bodily temple of the Holy Ghost ("what? know ye not that your body is the temple of the Holy Ghost which is in you?"), it is a fleshly temple, not a spiritual one. The whole meaning of being born again and becoming identified with the death of Christ is that His life might be manifested in our mortal flesh. When we are born from above the life of the Son of God is born in us, and the perfection of that life enables us not only to 'make out' what the will of God is, but to carry out His will in our natural human life.

TEMPTATION IN PARADISE

Chapter iii

There is something inconceivable to us in Adam's relationship to God, he saw God as simply as we see one another—"And they heard the voice ('sound', R.V. marg.) of the Lord God walking in the garden in the cool of the day:" (v. 8). Until Adam fell, he was not *interested in* God, he was *one with* God in communion—a man is never interested in that which he is; when Adam fell, he became so appallingly interested in God that he was afraid of Him—"and the man and his wife hid themselves from the presence of the Lord God amongst the trees of the garden." Sin finds us severed from God and interested only in anything we can be told about Him, consequently there is an element of fear; when we become children of God, there is no fear. As long as a child has not done wrong he enjoys perfect freedom and confidence towards his parents, but let him disobey, and the one he disobeys becomes someone in whom he is interested, with an element of fear. Conscious piety springs from being interested in God—'I want to know whether I am right with God'; if you are right with God, you are so one with Him that you are unconscious of it, the relationship is deeper than consciousness because you are being disposed by the very nature of God.

When the Apostle Paul talks of a man sinning: "*Therefore, as through one man sin entered into the world,*" remember who it is he refers to, viz., not to a

6

being like you or me, but to the great Federal Head of
the human race. Sin is not part of human nature as
God designed it, it is extraneous. The Bible looks on
sin, not as a disease, but as red-handed rebellion
against the domination of the Creator. The essence of
sin is—'I won't allow anybody to "boss" me saving
myself', and it may manifest itself in a morally good
man as well as in a morally bad man. Sin has not to do
with morality or immorality, it has to do with my
claim to my right to myself, a deliberate and emphatic
independence of God, though I veneer it over with
Christian phraseology. If, as a saint, I allow this spirit
to get back into me, I become the embodiment of
heaven and hell in conflict.

"And the Lord God commanded the man, saying,
Of every tree in the garden thou mayest freely eat:
but of the tree of the knowledge of good and evil thou
shalt not eat of it: *for in the day that thou eatest thereof
thou shalt surely die*" (ch. ii. 17). "And the serpent
said unto the woman, *Ye shall not surely die*" (ch. iii. 4).
Eve finds that what Satan told her is true, death does
not strike them all at once: but its possibility has come
in. Death has secretly begun. We transgress a law of
God and expect an experience akin to death, but
exactly the opposite happens, we feel enlarged, more
broad-minded, more tolerant of evil, but we are more
powerless; knowledge which comes from eating of the
tree of the knowledge of good and evil, instead of
instigating to action, paralyses.

"For the wages of sin is death;"—man becomes
subject to death, not because he is a finite being, but
because of sin. Whenever a man touches sin, death
is the inevitable result, it is the way God has con-
stituted him; when he is 'alive' in sin, he is 'dead' to
God. "And you did He quicken, when ye were dead

through your trespasses and sins" (Ephesians ii. 1). What every human being inherits is not *punishment* for sin but the *disposition* of sin which "entered into the world through one man, and death through sin; and so death passed upon all men for that all have sinned". Death was not in God's purpose for man. When we are born again we have exactly the experience of going through death. "Thou canst not see My face: for man shall not see Me and live" (Exodus xxxiii. 20)—and yet we do see God and live, but we only see God by going through death. I must die, die right out to my claim to my right to myself, and receive the gift of eternal life, which is 'the gift of God through Jesus Christ our Lord'.

"And the man said, The woman Thou gavest to be with me, she gave me of the tree, and I did eat;" Adam does not blame himself; neither does Eve blame herself: "And the woman said, The serpent beguiled me, and I did eat." They both evade the moral truth. Verbal truth is rarely moral truth. It takes a long time to bring me to the place where I will blame myself. Adam *admits*, but there is no confession, he implies rather that God is to blame—'You should not have put me in a position where I could disobey; I don't deny I did wrong, but remember the extenuating circumstances, You shouldn't be so stern and holy'. That is the first manifestation of the spirit of anarchy. The diabolical nature of sin is that it hates God, because when I am face to face with the holiness of God I know there is no escape, consequently there is nothing the natural heart of man hates like a holy God. We don't live deep enough down to realize this. 'If only God would not be so holy as my conscience tells me He is'. It is a mixed-up certainty, I know I am not right with God and I don't want to be—and yet I do.

8

I will do anything rather than take the responsibility on myself for having done wrong: or if I do accept the responsibility, I defy God to readjust me, the one is as bad as the other. I either refuse to say I have sinned, or I admit I have sinned and refuse to let God save me; I won't allow God to have the last word; I have the last word and intend to stick to it. That is the attitude of the devil. "If we *confess* our sins, . . ." says the Apostle John. Whenever conviction of sin comes, out into the light with it, confess it, because when I realize the shame of it and accept God's forgiveness, there is an inwrought energy brought back in place of the energy which went out in the sin; with the majority of us that energy is lost, it does not come back in "the fruits of repentance."

"And the Lord said unto the serpent, I will put enmity between thee and the woman, and between thy seed and her seed: . . ." (*v.* 15). God does not deal with Satan direct, man must deal with Satan because man is responsible for his introduction. That is why God became Incarnate. Put it in any other way—why God could banish Satan in two seconds; but it is man who, through the Redemption, is to overcome Satan, and much more than overcome him, he is to do that which will exhibit the perfect fulfilment of this prophecy. Jesus Christ, the last Adam, took on Him our human form, and it is through His seed in that human form that Satan is to be overcome. "And the God of peace shall bruise Satan under your feet shortly" (Romans xvi. 20). Everything that Satan and sin have marred, God holds in an unimpaired state for every son of man who will come to Him by the way back which Jesus Christ has made.

9

MESSAGE OF GOD ON SIN

Chapter iv

(1) "Sin Coucheth at the Door:" (*v.* 7)

"And it came to pass, when they were in the field, that Cain rose up against his brother, and slew him" (*v.* 8).

No man can murder his brother who has not first murdered God in himself. Cain's crime is more than murdering his brother, it is a deeper crime within that crime, viz., the putting up of his whole nature against God, and, finally, accusing God for his punishment—'Of course, my sin is unpardonable if You are a holy God, but You are to blame for being a holy God'.

"And the Lord said unto Cain, Why art thou wroth? and why is thy countenance fallen? If thou doest well, shalt thou not be accepted?" (*vv.* 6–7). These verses present God doing for Cain what He did for Adam and Eve—giving him a Divine opportunity for repentance. Remorse is never repentance, remorse is the rebellion of man's own pride which will not agree with God's judgment on sin but accuses God because He has made His laws too stern and holy. Adam and Eve *acknowledged* their sin although they never *confessed* it. Cain evades acknowledgment; first, he lies to God, then he becomes scornful of God—"And the Lord said unto Cain, Where is Abel thy brother? And he said, I know not: am I my brother's keeper?" Sin in Adam and Eve revealed itself as envy of God (see ch. iii. 5); in Cain it advances to envy of his brother—"And the Lord had respect unto Abel and his offering: but unto Cain and his offering He had not respect. And Cain was very wroth, and his countenance fell." Personal vindictive rage is the spirit of murder. " . . . not as Cain was of the evil one, and slew his brother. And wherefore slew he him? Because his works were evil, and his brother's righteous." "Whosoever hateth his brother is a murderer." (1 John iii. 12, 15.)

"And He said, What hast thou done? the voice of thy brother's blood crieth unto Me from the ground" (*v.* 10). Murder may be done in a hundred and one ways, think of the number of voices that cry unto God to-day from men who have been murdered in civilized life. The cry of every murdered innocence, every perverted right, is in the ear of God, and in this sense the blood of Abel still speaks and will never be silenced.

(2) THE SOLITARINESS OF GUILT (*vv.* 11–15)

"And now cursed art thou from the ground, . . . a fugitive and a wanderer shalt thou be in the earth" (*vv.* 11, 12).

Beware of speaking of *reaction* when God says *retribution*. The man who has done wrong has such a guilty conscience that he imagines everything is against him: everything *is* against him—God is against him, every bit of earth is against him; he stands absolutely alone. Nothing associates itself with the sinner saving his sin. Once sin enters in, you are out of gear with God morally and with the universe physically.

"And Cain said unto the Lord, My punishment is greater than I can bear. Behold, thou hast driven me out this day from the face of the ground; and from thy face shall I be hid; and I shall be a fugitive and a wanderer in the earth;" (*vv.* 13–14).

11

Cain takes God's punishment, which is His mercy, and perverts it into a penal decree making it impossible for him to come back. He entrenches himself in despair as a garment and spits back accusations against God—'See what You have done; I can't get back'. When we are punished by God for wrong-doing our attitude is apt to be—'Oh well, it's no use trying to do any better, God has sent me from His presence, and I can't get back, I can do as I like now'. Beware of making the despairing-sulk complaint, which is found in all of us, a threatening accusation against God. God can never forgive despair. The door is always open to God until I shut it. God never shuts it; I shut it, then I lose the key and say, 'It's all up; whatever I do now God is entirely to blame'.

Look for these things inside yourself; if you don't find them there, you are a humbug to find them outside you. Never disassociate yourself from anything any human being has ever done, that is the delusion of a moral lunatic. God will give you such a knowledge of yourself that you won't be able to say, 'I don't know how anyone could do that', you will know humiliatingly before God how the vilest crime could be committed. You won't say, 'But I could never do that'; you could. Any human being can do what any human being has ever done. When you see a criminal and feel instantly, 'How horrible and vile that man is', it is a sure sign that the Lord is not in you; if He is in you, you will not only feel how horrible and vile he is, you will say, 'But for God, I am that, and much worse'. But don't use it as a pious phrase; if you don't mean it, never say it.

"And Cain went out from the presence of the Lord, and dwelt in the land of Nod," ("That is Wandering" R.V. marg.) (iv. 16).

Cain had no rest anywhere, the earth spurned him, therefore he went into the land of Wandering and constructed his own world. Men who have sinned and maintain themselves in their sin cannot endure themselves on God's earth, so they must make a world of their own and put it on God's earth. There is no place for sin on God's earth.

". . . and he builded a city," (v. 17).

The first civilization was founded by a murderer, and the whole basis of civilized life is a vast, complicated, more or less gilded-over system of murder. We find it more conducive to human welfare not to murder men outright, we do it by a system of competition. It is ingrained in our thinking that competition and rivalry are essential to the carrying on of civilized life; that is why Jesus Christ's statements seem wild and ridiculous. They are the statements either of a madman or of God Incarnate. To carry out the Sermon on the Mount is frankly impossible to anyone but a fool, and who is the fool? The man who has been born again and who dares to carry out in his individual life the teaching of Jesus. And what will happen? The inevitable result, not the success he would otherwise have. A hard saying, but true.

THE EVOLUTION OF DEPRAVITY

Chapter vi. 1-7

(1) THE FLOODS OF ELEMENTAL SIN

"And the Lord saw that the wickedness of man was great in the earth, and that every imagination of the thoughts of his heart was only evil continually" (*v.* 5).

Depravity must be taken to mean much more than going wrong, it means rather to be so established in the wrong that the result is a real pleasure in it. There is an inspiration in choosing to do wrong, it means a simplification of the life. Immediately you choose to do wrong you are not only conscious that you are without excuse, you become brazenly fixed in the wrong; that is the characteristic of the devil. The revelation the Bible makes is not that men are getting worse, but that men are damnable—consequently they are saveable; the system of things he lives in may get worse, but a man can't be worse than damnable. If the mind of man persistently tries to remove the possibility of damnation he destroys the justice of God, destroys his own manhood, and leaves in its place an evolving animal-life to which God is not necessary.

Matthew xv. 19 ("For out of the heart come forth evil thoughts, . . ." See also Jeremiah xvii. 9, "the heart is deceitful above all things, and desperately wicked: who can know it?") refers to the depravity of the human heart apart from God. The elemental fountain of depravity is there, the reason it is not manifested to my consciousness is either sheer ignorance by reason of a refusal to accept Jesus Christ's diagnosis, or because I have been saved and sanctified by God's mighty grace. According to our Lord "these things" are in the mother-heart, that deepest seat of moral character that lies below the conscious, the conscious thought, and still more the conscious purpose. When God's Spirit comes in and opens from underneath our consciousness the abyss we are on, the only thing to do is to completely surrender to Him, and the abyss is closed for ever. It is entire rightness with Jesus Christ alone that prevents elemental depravity working in the heart and out into deeds. If I trust Jesus Christ's diagnosis and hand over the keeping of my heart to Him, I need never know in conscious experience what depravity is, but if I trust in my innocent ignorance I am likely one of these days to turn a corner and find that what He said is true. When the crisis comes and men find that what they took to be their innocent heart is really a sink of iniquity, they would be the first to say, 'Why did not God tell us?' 'Why were we not warned?' We are warned, perfectly clearly, in order that we need never go through the terrible experience of knowing the truth of what Jesus said— *"For from within, out of the heart of men, evil thoughts proceed . . .",* that is the marvellous mercy of God. Jesus Christ's teaching never beats about the bush. Our stupidity is to believe only what we are conscious of and not the revelation He has made. Instead of its being a sign of good taste, it is a sign of shocking unbelief when men won't face what Jesus Christ has put so plainly, so unmistakably plainly, so brutally plainly at times, about the human heart. Again, let me urge you, never trust your innocent ignorance when Jesus Christ's statements contradict it.

15

Whenever any choice of ours is based on implicit disregard of God, we are depraved, and this possibility remains in every saint. 'Now I am saved and sanctified all I choose is sure to be right'; not by any means. 'All I think is sure to be right', not so; if our choices and our thinking do not spring from the basis of a determined recognition of God, we are depraved, no matter what our experience spiritually.

(2) THE FOUNDATION OF ETERNAL SALVATION

"and it repented the Lord that He had made men on the earth, and it grieved Him at His heart" (v. 6).

An unemotional love is inconceivable. Love for the good must involve displeasure and grief for the evil. God is not an almighty sultan reigning aloof, He is right in the throes of life, and it is there that emotion shows itself.

"And it repented the Lord . . ." God does not repent like a man, He repents like God, that is, without change of plan or purpose. "God is not a man, that He should lie; neither the son of man, that He should repent: hath He said, and shall He not do it?" (Numbers xxiii. 19.) If God were to say of any sin, 'Oh well, he didn't mean it, I will let it go', that would be a change in God's purpose. If God overlooked one sin in me, He would cease to be God. The 'repenting' of God in individual cases means that God remains true to His purpose and must mean my condemnation, and my condemnation causes Him grief and agony. It is not that God won't overlook wrong, it is that He cannot, His very love forbids it. When I am saved by God's almighty grace I realize that I am delivered completely from what He has

16

condemned—and *that* is salvation; I don't palliate it any longer, but agree with God's verdict on it on the Cross. At the back of all the condemnation of God put 'Calvary'.

THE CALL OF THE FORLORN-HOPE

Chapter vi. 8–22

"But Noah found grace in the eyes of the Lord. Noah was a righteous man, and perfect ("blameless" R.V. marg.) in his generations: Noah walked with God" (*vv.* 8–9).

(1) "NOAH FOUND GRACE"

Grace is the overflowing immeasurable favour of God; God cannot withhold, the only thing that keeps back His grace and favour is our sin and perversity. —"*Noah walked with God.*" To walk with God means the perpetual realization of the nature of faith, viz., that it must be tried or it is mere fancy; faith un-tried has no character-value for the individual. There is nothing akin to faith in the natural world, defiant pluck and courage is not faith; it is the *trial* of faith that is "much more precious than of gold", and the trial of faith is never without the essentials of temptation. It is to be questioned whether any child of God ever gets through the trial of his faith without at some stage being horror-stricken; what God does comes as a stinging blow, and he feels the suffering is not deserved, yet, like Job, he will neither listen to nor tell lies about God. Spiritual character is only made by standing loyal to God's character no matter what distress the trial of faith brings. The distress and agony the prophets experienced was the agony of believing God when everything that was happening contradicted what they proclaimed Him to be; there was nothing to prove that God was just and true, but everything to prove the opposite. The forlorn-hope aspect is the best, perhaps the only idea, for the godly in Time: all that has been built up on the basis of personal faith in God is contradicted by the immediate present, and it is the man who does not believe in God who has the safest, best time of it in the immediate present. The Bible is full of this attitude to things (e.g., Psalm lxxiii). It is when we forget this aspect of godliness that we cease to walk with God and only pay court visits to Him; we cease to be His children. To walk with God means walking apart from ultimate godless reliances. There is no such thing as a *venture* of faith, only a determined *walk with God* by faith.

"And Noah begat three sons," (*v.* 9). Noah's sons are mentioned because in them the continuance of the human race is secure. If you are a snob you won't like the Bible genealogies because they have no respect for the aristocratic notion. Snobbery is the insistence on going far enough back—but not too far!

(2) "MY SPIRIT SHALL NOT STRIVE WITH MAN FOR EVER"

"And God looked upon the earth, and, behold, it was corrupt; for all flesh had corrupted His way upon the earth. . . . and, behold, I will destroy them with the earth." ("from the earth". A.V. marg.) (*vv.* 11–13).

It is God's long-suffering patience ultimately coming to the conclusion that He must let the full destruction of His righteousness have its way. "And God looked" —as if until now God had looked away, giving time through Enoch and Methuselah and Lamech, then suddenly He looks, and destruction swift and almighty comes and there is no reprieve, it means judgment, a final sentence. The pronouncement of coming doom is a combining of judgment and deliverance. When God's limit is reached He destroys the unsaveable and liberates the saveable; consequently judgment days are the great mercy of God because they separate between good and evil, between right and wrong. Salvation to be experimental in me is always a judgment inasmuch as it is concerned with some kind of separation. 'The Cross condemns men to salvation'. I remain indifferent to the Cross until I realize by the conviction of the Spirit of God that there are certain things in me which are damnable. I can always know the kind of disposition I have got by the sword God brings against me, I may plead and pray, but He is merciless, He saves me "so as by fire". When once I am willing to agree with God's condemnation in the Cross on those things, God in His infinite mercy, by bringing His judgment, saves. It is not judgment inaugurating salvation, but judgment that *is* salvation. The same with nations, and with the human race.

(3) "MAKE THEE AN ARK"

The ark stands as a reminder that nothing *is* until it is. Whenever we say a thing is impossible the reason is twofold—either our prejudices don't wish it to be, or we say it is too wonderful to be possible. From the building of the ark on, just make quite sure a thing is impossible, and God does it. God can only do the impossible. In the realm of our human possible we don't need God, common-sense is our God; we don't pray to God, we pray to an erection of our common-sense. It is God who is the Architect of salvation, therefore salvation is not a common-sense design; what we have to do is to get inside that salvation. If I put my faith in any erection of my own, my vows and decisions, my consecration, I am building

20

something for myself; I must co-operate with God in His plan of salvation. Picture Noah sitting down and saying, 'God has given me a wonderful plan, I will watch and see it grow'! *"Thus Noah did: according to all that God commanded him"* (v. 22).

"And I, behold, I do bring the flood of waters upon the earth, to destroy all flesh, . . ." (v. 17). The initiative springs from the Mind of Almighty God, *"And I, behold, I do bring . . ."* it is not the natural consequence of cause and effect. "But I will establish My covenant with thee;" with the new humanity after the flood. The ' afterwards' of God is never disconnected with the 'before' of His promise, and God's 'afterwards' is more than the fulfilment of His promise, it is the re-expression of the fulfilment of the 'before' of His purpose by my coming into living relationship with Him, if I will.

THE DARK OF FAITH

Chapters vii–ix

"And the flood was forty days upon the earth, . . . and all
the high mountains that were under the whole heaven were
covered . . .: and Noah only was left, and they that were with
him in the ark. And the waters prevailed upon the earth an
hundred and fifty days" (ch. vii. 17–24).

The ark itself is submerged, saving the top of it, no
foothold anywhere. God removed hope from anywhere but Himself. That is a picture of the Kingdom
of God in this dispensation, it appears to be completely
submerged, yet those very things which look as if they
were going to smash it are the things God uses to
preserve it.

(1) THE EXPRESS COVENANT

"But I will establish My covenant with thee;" (ch. vi.
18).

"And God remembered Noah" (ch. viii. 1). This
does not mean that God had forgotten Noah; the
remembrances of God are sure to those who will put
their trust in Him. It is significant to note that whenever the Bible uses terms such as 'repent', 'remember',
'forsake', 'love', in connection with God, their human
meaning does not apply, e.g., the love of God can only
be illustrated by the character of God.

"And after the end of an hundred and fifty days the
waters decreased . . .'(vv. 3–8). The 'at last' of God is
never an anticlimax, it always exceeds any possible

human forecast. We must be careful never to compromise over any promise of God when by reason of human limitation there has been only a partial fulfilment. Such a compromise is easily detected whenever you feel, 'Oh well, I suppose that is all God meant'. Every word God has spoken will be absolutely fulfilled; to climb down from that confidence is to be disloyal to God. Beware, though, of inferring because no good word of God will fail, that I personally will necessarily partake in its fulfilment; I assuredly will not unless I have come into vital relationship with God by determined faith.

"And he stayed yet another seven days" (vv. 10–14). These verses indicate the prominent characteristic of Noah, viz., the humility of patience. Patience is not the same as endurance because the heart of endurance is frequently stoical, whereas the heart of patience is a blazing love that sees intuitively and waits God's time in perfect confidence. It is impossible to be patient and proud because pride weakens into lust, and lust is essentially impatient. Noah stands for all time as the embodiment of the patience of hope.

"And God spake to Noah, saying, Go forth of the ark, . . . and Noah went forth, . . ." (vv. 15–18). As Noah went into the ark at the command of God, so at the command of God he goes forth of the ark. Had Noah been a fanatic, when God said, "Go forth of the ark", he would have said, 'No, God said "Come thou into the ark", and this must be the voice of the devil'. There is always the danger of becoming a fanatical adherent to what God has said instead of adhering to God who said it. Noah waited God's time to go out of the ark. The only way to wait for the Second Coming is to watch that you do what you should do so that *when* He comes is a matter of indifference. It is the attitude of a child, certain that God knows what He is about. When the Lord does come it will be as natural as breathing. God never does anything hysterical, and He never produces hysterics.

(2) THE ABIDING RELATIONSHIP

"And God spake unto Noah, and to his sons with him, saying, and I, behold, I establish My covenant with you, and with your seed after you; . . ." (ch. ix. 8–17).

God cannot do certain things without the co-operation of man. We continually ask, 'Why doesn't God do the thing instead of waiting for me?' He cannot. It is the same problem as the difference between God's order and His permissive will. His permissive will allows the devil to do his worst and allows me to sin as I choose, until I choose to resist the devil, quit sinning, and come to God in the right relationship of a covenant with Him through Jesus Christ. It is God's will that human beings should get into moral relationship with Him and His covenants are for that purpose. 'Why doesn't God save me?' He has saved me, but I have not entered into relationship with Him. 'Why doesn't God do this and that?' He has done it, the point is—will I step into covenant relationship with Him? All the great blessings of God are finished and complete, but they are not mine until I enter into relationship with Him on the basis of His covenant. Salvation is not an edict of God; salvation is something wrought out on the human plane through God becoming Man. Waiting for God is incarnate unbelief, it means I have no faith in Him, I want Him to do something in me that I may trust in that. God won't do it, because that is not the basis of the God-and-man relationship. Man has to go out of himself in his covenant with God as God goes out of Himself in His covenant with man. It is a question of faith in God, the rarest thing, we have faith only in our feelings. I don't believe God unless He will give me something in my hand whereby I may know I have it, then I say, 'Now I believe'. There is no faith there. "*Look unto Me*, and be ye saved," God says. When I have really transacted business with God on His covenant and have let go entirely, there is no sense of merit, no human ingredient in it at all, but a complete, overwhelming sense of having been brought into union with God, and the whole thing is transfigured with peace and joy.

Chapters xii–xxv are dealt with in the book entitled "Not Knowing Whither."

ABIDING FACTORS

Chapter xxvi. 1–12

(1) COMMENCEMENT OF DESTITUTION

"And there was a famine in the land, beside the first famine that was in the days of Abraham" (*v.* 1).

Isaac's history commences with the same trial as Abraham's, viz., a famine in the land. Abraham acted according to his own wits, not according to his faith in God: "and Abram went down to Egypt to sojourn there; for the famine was sore in the land"—destitution in the very land of promise. Watch the destitution of wits that follows quickly on the heels of a Divine revelation. Whenever you get a revelation from God you will be starved at once, starved, that is, in your wits, you can see no way out. Every time your wits compete with the worship of God you had better take a strong dose of Isaiah xxx. 15–16—"In returning and rest shall ye be saved; in quietness and in confidence shall be your strength: and ye would not." Beware of restlessness and wits persuading you that God has made a blunder—'God would never allow me to fall sick after giving me such a blessing'; but He has! No matter what revelations God has made to you, there will be destitution so far as the physical apprehension of things is concerned—God gives you a revelation that He will provide, then He provides nothing and you begin to realize that there is a famine, of food, or of clothes, or money, and your common-sense as well as other people's says, 'Abandon your faith in God, do this, and that'. Do it at your peril. Watch where destitution comes; if it comes on the heels of a time of quiet confidence in God, then thank Him for it and stay starving and He will bring a glorious issue.

(2) COMMAND IN TRIAL

"And the Lord appeared unto him, and said, Go not down into Egypt; dwell in the land which I shall tell thee of:" (v. 2).

The command to Abraham was to depart; the command to Isaac is to remain. When the 'Isaac' life of quietness and confidence in God is born of the 'Abraham' life of strenuous separation, don't make any more separations, just be still, and know that God is God. Those who educate you in the things of God will be the first to pull you back when you obey the voice which came through them. God taught you the right thing through them, and now you are obeying they come in with their own wits and say, 'Of course we didn't mean you should do that'; but God did. Beware of mixing quietness and confidence with other people's wits.

(3) CONFIRMATION OF TRUTH (vv. 3-5)

". . . because that Abraham obeyed My voice, and kept My charge, My commandments, My statutes and My laws" (v. 5).

Isaac is promised Divine blessing and protection because of God's oath which He swore to Abraham on account of his obedience. Abraham's obedience was far from perfect, but its great characteristic was its unreservedness. Abandon in the profound sense is of infinitely more value than personal holiness. Personal holiness brings the attention to bear on my own whiteness, I dare not be indiscreet, or unreserved, I dare not do anything in case I incur a speck. God can't bless that sort of thing, it is as unlike His own character as could be. The holiness produced through the indwelling of His Son in me is a holiness which is never conscious of itself. There are some people in whom you cannot find a speck and yet they are not abundantly blessed of God, while others make grave indiscretions and get marvellously blessed; the reason being that the former have become devotees of personal holiness, conscientious to a degree; the latter are marked by abandonment to God. Whatever centres attention on anything other than our Lord Himself will always lead astray. The only way to be kept cleansed is by walking in the light, as God is in the light. Only as we walk in that light is the holiness of Jesus Christ not only imputed, but imparted, to us.

Abraham's aberrations sprang not from disobedience, but from trusting in his own wits. Directly God's command was made known to him, he obeyed; when there was no command he was inclined to trust in his wits, and that is where he went wrong. It is never right to do wrong in order that right may come, although it may seem justifiable from every standard saving one. In the long run you can never produce right by doing wrong, yet we will always try to do it unless we believe what the Bible says. If I tell a lie in order to bring about the right, I prove to my own conviction that I do not believe the One at the back of the universe is truthful. Judge everything in the light of Jesus Christ, who is The Truth, and you will never do the wrong thing however right it looks.

THE TENDER GRACE

Chapter xxvi. 13–25

The only right a Christian has is the right to give up his rights. This is the tender grace which is usually looked upon as an exhibition of lack of gumption. The embarrassing thing about Christian graces is that immediately you imitate them they become nauseating, because conscious imitation implies an affected preference for certain qualities, and we produce frauds by a spurious piety. All the qualities of a godly life are characteristic of the life of God; you cannot imitate the life of God unless you have it, then the imitation is not conscious, but the unconscious manifestation of the real thing. 'Pi' people try to produce the life of God by sheer imitation; they pretend to be sweet when really they are bitter. The life of God has no pretence, and when His life is in you, you do not pretend to feel sweet, you *are* sweet.

(1) THE EXTERNAL GREATNESS OF ISAAC

"And the man waxed great, and grew more and more until he became very great:" (*v.* 13).

Isaac never became great in the way that Abraham did, his greatness is of a different order. Abraham was not only a great man of God, he was a great *man*. Some lives exhibit grand characteristics and yet there are curious defects; the only standard for judging the saint is Jesus Christ, not saintly qualities. Beware of the snare of taking people as types; no one is a type of anything, he may recall a particular type, but he is always something other than the type. If Abraham is taken as the type of a saint you get embarrassed because of the things in him which are not saintly. We are always inclined to remain true to our own ideas of a person, it does not matter what the facts are, we interpret all that he does according to our idea of him. If I accept you as an expression of my idea of you, I will be unjust to you as a fact; I make you either better or worse than you are, I never hit just 'you' until I learn to accept facts as facts.

(2) THE EXTRAORDINARY GENTLENESS OF ISAAC (vv. 14–26)

"And Isaac's servants digged in the valley, and found there a well of springing ("living" R.V. marg.) water. And the herdsmen of Gerar strove with Isaac's herdsmen, saying, The water is ours: and he called the name of the well Esek ("That is, Contention" R.V. marg.); because they contended with him" (v. 20).

The strife arose around a well of living water, and Isaac let them have it, that is, he refused to drink of the water of 'Contention'. Whenever a doctrinal well becomes 'Esek', give it up; your life with God is more precious than proving you are right doctrinally. It is at the peril of your communion with God that you contend about a doctrine. "And they digged another well, and they strove for that also:" And Isaac surrendered it, calling it Sitnah, "That is, Enmity." (R.V. marg.) It is a great sign of grace not to break your heart because you cannot drink of the water of 'Enmity'. "And he removed from thence, and digged another well, and for that they strove not: and he called the name of it Rehoboth; ("That is, Broad places, or Room" R.V. marg.) and he said, For now the Lord hath made room for us, and we shall be fruitful in the land."

"And the Lord appeared to him the same night, and said, I am the God of Abraham thy father; fear not, for I am with thee, and will bless thee, and multiply thy seed for My servant Abraham's sake." Isaac has come to a broad place and God appears to him, and for the first time the grand phrase, *"I am the God of Abraham"* appears. "And he builded an altar there, and called upon the name of the Lord."

When you stand up for another who has been grossly wronged and your stand to be of any avail must have the co-operation of the wronged one, there is nothing more maddening than to find that he is without any resentment. That must have been the heart-breaking embarrassment to the disciples over our Lord; they had built up their own ideas as to how He was going to bring in His Kingdom and they were prepared to fight for Him, then they saw Jesus meekly give Himself up to the power of the world, He did nothing whatever to assert His rights. In the Christian life the problem arises not from the world, which says you are a fool, but from your friends who are prepared to stand up for you.

Inoffensiveness, which is one of the chief characteristics of Isaac, usually means to our natural minds a quality unsuited to a strong personality. We have to bear in mind that the life of our Lord portrayed just this characteristic of inoffensiveness: "As a lamb that is led to the slaughter, and as a sheep that before her shearers is dumb; yea, He opened not His mouth." "He was crucified through weakness," and, "we also are weak in Him." Anything to do with meekness and submissiveness is antagonistic to robust human nature. Our impatience gets beyond its limit because of the characteristics Jesus Christ insists upon: "*Learn of Me; for I am meek and lowly in heart, . . .*" The natural heart builds on adventure, recklessness, independence, impulse; the characteristics God prizes are produced only in the son of sacrifice. Natural inoffensiveness may be the weakness of constitutional timidity; supernatural inoffensiveness is almighty strength scorning to use the weapons of the flesh. Inoffensiveness is self-control indwelt by the Holy Ghost, "the fruit of the Spirit is . . . self-control".

(3) The Eternal and the Haphazard (*vv.* 28–33)

"Let there now be an oath betwixt us and thee, and let us make a covenant with thee; . . . And he made them a feast and they did eat and drink. And they rose up betimes in the morning, and sware one to another: . . . And it came to pass the same day, that Isaac's servants came, and told him concerning the well which they had digged, and said unto him, We have found water. And he called it Shibah: therefore the name of the city is Beer-sheba unto this day"—well of the oath.

All the transactions entered into by both Abraham and Isaac, no matter how temporary or casual, were based on their relationship to God, that is, they used their wits in their worship of Him. This recognition of God began to be lost during Jacob's life, and the children of Israel went on ignoring it until they came to establish all their transactions on their own wits. Our Lord warns against taking an oath (*see* Matthew v. 33–5), because in the sight of God an oath means the recognition of God in the most temporary transaction. In the Old Testament, and in the record of the Resurrection, we find the temporary matter of eating and drinking put on the eternal foundation of relationship to God. The things which can be most easily ridiculed are the things that have most of God in them.

32

A saint can be ridiculed because he sees haphazard happenings in the light of the eternal—'The Lord guided me here, and there'. The fact that a man who is a fraud says the same thing as a saint is proof that he is counterfeiting something which is real. No actual fact has its right name unless you can worship God in it. Remember, whatever happens, God is there. It is easy to fix your mind on God in a lecture, but a different matter to fix your mind on Him when there is a war on. You never get at God by blinking facts, but only by naming Him in the facts; whether they are devilish or not, say, 'Lord, I thank Thee that Thou art here'.

PLANS AND PROVIDENCE

Chapter xxvii

"And Rebekah heard when Isaac spake to Esau her son" (*v. 5*).

Plans arise from the human 'must'—the imperative demand of my own undisciplined nature which makes me feel, 'I must do something; God is no use here'. God rarely rebukes us for our impulsive plans because those plans work their own distress. Plans made apart from trusting God's wisdom are rotten. *Providence* arises from God's majesty. The wisdom of God can never be according to man's understanding, and in our regenerated lives while we are 'climbing the slow ascensions' of our Heavenly Father's wisdom, He engineers our circumstances by His providence and puts within our inmost soul the childlike joy of confidence in Himself. It is always easier not to trust; if I can work the thing out for myself then I am not going to trust in God. I work out a plan whereby I say God must do the thing and I force His hand along certain lines, and when He does what I said I knew He would do, for an exhilarating moment I think I have made Him do it! Then I find I am to be punished for everything I tried to make Him do, though it looks as if my wrong had brought about His good. Beware of egging God on; possess your soul in patience.

Always beware when you can reasonably account to yourself for the action you are about to take, because the source of such clear reasoning is the enthroning of human understanding. It is this element in the personal life of a Christian that fights longest and to the last against the enthronement of Jesus Christ as Lord and Master. 'Supposing I do say I will go to the foreign field, what about this, and that?' 'I want a reasonable explanation'. As long as you argue like that it is all up with devotion to Jesus Christ. He will have no influence over you until your plan is worked out because you have put your own wits on the throne. The reason we know so little about God's wisdom is that we will only trust Him as far as we can work things out according to our own reasonable common-sense.

(1) Sensitiveness to Divinely Shaped Ends (*vv.* 6–17)

"Now therefore, my son, obey my voice according to that which I command thee . . ." (*vv.* 8–17).

Still waters run deep, but an able woman is deeper. Abraham made the supreme blunder of trying to help God fulfil His promise; Rebekah repeats the blunder. A woman with a sense of values in the end to be achieved cares nothing about herself in the accomplishing of that end. "And his mother said unto him, Upon me be thy curse, my son: only obey my voice, . . . " When a virtuous woman does wrong she does it with all the characteristic of her virtue transferred to the deception; Rebekah carried out her deception as though she were called and inspired of God to do it. In such a case the sin is not the outcome of impulse, but the deliberate perversion of integrity. In individual experience no one person is ever entirely to blame—'my father is to blame, my mother, my heredity', everybody and everything but myself. It is

impossible for human wisdom to apportion the blame.
Remember the one fact more which God alone knows.

(2) SCHEMES OF DISCREET EXPECTATIONS (vv. 18-25)

"And Rebekah took the goodly raiment of Esau her elder
son, which were with her in the house, and put them upon
Jacob her younger son: . . ." (vv. 15-17).

This is the first pious lie enacted in the Bible.
Rebekah's motive was born of the oracles of God—
". . . and the elder shall serve the younger" (ch. xxv.
23): her act was entirely wrong; she enacted a lie in
order to help God carry out His purpose. This is very
different from the lie told for our own ends.

Jacob's enunciation of the lie—"And Jacob said
unto his father, I am Esau thy firstborn;" is expressive
fundamentally, not of self-seeking, but of devotion to
his mother, consequently there is no hesitation or
bravado because he is not yet so conscious as he will
be of what he is doing. Beware of obeying anyone
else's obedience to God because it means you are
shirking responsibility yourself.

"And his father Isaac said unto him, Come near now,
and kiss me, my son . . . Be lord over thy brethren,
and let thy mother's sons bow down to thee:" The
whole lie is now enacted, and Jacob enters into the
fullness of the blessing. God fore-ordained that the
blessing should come to Jacob, but it was not part of
that fore-ordination that Jacob should enter into the
blessing in the way he did. There are experiences in
human lives which are not part of God's purpose, but
the result of human perversity. Remember, trust in
God does not mean that God will explain His solutions
to us, it means that we are perfectly confident in God,
and when we do see the solution we find it to be in
accordance with all that Jesus Christ revealed of His

character. It is nonsense to imagine that God expects me to discern all that is clear to His own mind, all He asks of me is to maintain perfect confidence in Himself. Faith springs from the indwelling of the life of God in me.

THE LONE QUEST

Chapter xxviii

(1) THE DISCIPLINE OF THE UNCHANGING DESTINY (*vv.* 1–9)

"And God Almighty bless thee, . . . that thou mayest inherit the land of thy sojournings, which God gave unto Abraham" (*vv.* 3–4).

Jacob's destiny had nothing to do with his personal character, but his personal character had everything to do with the desperate discipline he went through. God's destiny for a life will be fulfilled though the details of the fulfilment are determined by the individual. The kind of discipline Jacob went through was determined by his perversity. The 'lone quest' is never pathetic unless, as in Jacob's case, it is mixed with cunning and sin in motive.

"Was not Esau Jacob's brother? saith the Lord: yet I loved Jacob; but Esau I hated" (Malachi i. 2–3). In all implicit matters intuition is of more avail than logic. Naturally, we are inclined to love Esau and dislike Jacob. The most undesirable person in later life is often the one who was most desirable when young. A chaotic young life is always the most satisfactory. ". . . yet I loved Jacob"—God loves the man who needs Him. Esau was satisfied with what he was; Jacob wanted more than he was. Esau never saw visions, never wrestled with angels, although God was as near to him as to Jacob. Esau refused to sacrifice anything to the spiritual; he could never think of anything but the present. He was willing to sell the promise of the future for a mess of pottage, and thereby he wronged himself far more than Jacob did.

(2) THE DREAM OF THE UNIMAGINED DIGNITY (vv. 10–22)

"And he dreamed, and behold a ladder set up on the earth, and the top of it reached to heaven; and behold the angels of God ascending and descending on it. And behold, the Lord stood above it ("beside him" R.V. marg.), and said, I am the Lord, the God of Abraham thy father, and the God of Isaac; the land whereon thou liest, to thee will I give it, and to thy seed; and thy seed shall be as the dust of the earth, and thou shalt spread abroad to the west, and to the east, and to the north, and to the south: and in thee and in thy seed shall all the families of the earth be blessed" (vv. 12–15).

Jacob's dream was a vision of the purpose of God for all the families of the earth. The destiny of the people known as 'Israel' is forecast in this one lonely man. God did not *select* this people, He *elected* them. God created them from Abraham to be His servants until through them every nation came to know who Jehovah was. They mistook the election of God's purpose to be the election of God's favouritism, and the story of their distress is due to their determination to use themselves for purposes other than God's. To this day they survive miraculously, the reason for their survival is the purpose of God to be fulfilled through them. They can still wait, still see visions of God, and the time is coming when God's promise shall be fulfilled materialistically. The prophecies are frequently taken as pictures of spiritual blessings; they are much more than that.

"And he dreamed, and behold a ladder set up on the earth, and the top of it reached to heaven." The ladder symbolizes communication between God and man.

39

The only Being in whom communication with God was never broken is the Lord Jesus Christ, and His claim is that through the Redemption He can put every one of us in the place where communication with God can be re-established. Paul's phrase 'in Christ'— the Mystical Christ, not the Historic Christ—is a revelation of the Redemption at work on our behalf. If I am 'in Christ' the angels of God are always ascending and descending on my behalf, and the voice that speaks is the voice of God. (Cf. John i. 51.)

Beware of having a measuring-rod for the Almighty, of tying God up in His own laws. This pre-Incarnate vision of God was given to such a man as Jacob was. It is dangerous to have the idea that we merit these things; immediately prayer or devotion is taken as the ground of God's blessing we are off the track. Prayer and devotion are simply the evidence that we are on God's plan; to be devoid of any sense of ill-being spiritually is a sign that we are not on God's plan. Jacob is the man who represents life as it is. The world is not made up of saints or of devils, but of people like you and me, and our real home is at the foot of the ladder with Jacob. Never say that God intends a man to have a domain of dreaming, mighty visions of God, and at the same time be dead towards God in his actual life. Jesus Christ claims that He can make the real and the actual one, as they were in His own life. When the vision comes it does not come to the 'Esau' type of man, he is so thick-hided that to talk to him about the nearness of God's presence is absurd, there is no meaning in it—that is absolutely true, there *is* no meaning in it, until he gets to the desolate spot. We cling to the certainty that the rational common-sense life is the right one; Jesus Christ stands for the fact that a life based on the Redemption is the only right one, consequently when a man shifts from the one to the other there is a period of desolation. Remember, there is a vast moral distance between Beth-el and Peniel.

(3) THE DEDICATION OF THE UNPARALLELED DAWN (vv. 16–20)

"And Jacob awaked out of his sleep, and he said, Surely the Lord is in this place; and I knew it not. And he was afraid, and said, How dreadful is this place! this is none other but the house of God, and this is the gate of heaven" (vv. 16–17).

"This place" means just where it is not within the bounds of imagination to infer that God would be. "And he called the name of that place Beth-el ("The house of God" R.V. marg.) because there God was revealed unto him." 'Every house of God is a gate of heaven where the impossible and the miraculous become the natural breath'. There is always an amazed surprise when we find what God brings with Him when He comes, He brings everything! (John xiv. 23).

It is in the dark night of the soul that the realization of God's presence breaks upon us: we never see God as long as, like Esau, we are perfectly satisfied with what we are. When I am certain that 'in me dwelleth no good thing', I begin to experience the miracle of seeing and hearing, not according to my senses, but according to the way the Holy Spirit interprets the word of God to me. Any number of people are happy without God, because happiness depends on not too profound an understanding of things; 'the god of this world hath blinded their minds', ("thoughts" R.V. marg. 2 Corinthians iv. 4). When the revelation of God's presence does come, it comes to those who are where Jacob was, in downright need and depression, knowing there is no

41

help anywhere saving in God. As long as there is any vestige of human sufficiency it is all up with the message of God as far as we are concerned.

When we come to consider it, the phrase, "the God of Jacob", is the greatest possible inspiration; it has in it the whole meaning of the Gospel of Jesus Christ, who said ". . . for I came not to call the righteous, but sinners." Had we been left with such phrases as 'the God of Joseph', or 'the God of Daniel', it would have spelt hopeless despair for most of us; but "the God of Jacob" means 'God is *my* God', the God not only of the noble character, but of the sneak. From the sneak to entire sanctification is the miracle of the grace of God.

LOVE

Chapter xxix

Love, more than any other experience in life, reveals the shallowness and the profundity, the hypocrisy and the nobility, of human nature. In dealing with all implicit things, such as love, there is a danger of being sentimentally consistent to a doctrine or an idea while the actual life is ignored; we forget that we have to live in this world as human beings. Consistency in doctrine ought to work out into expression in actual life, otherwise it produces the humbug in us; we have the jargon of the real thing, but actually we are not there. Anything that makes a man keep up a posture is not real; e.g., it is not true to say that an understanding of the doctrine of sanctification will lead you into the experience: doctrinal exposition comes after the experience in order to bring the actual life into perfect harmony with the marvel of the work of God's grace.

(1) GOD AND THE CULT OF THE PASSING MOMENT

"Then Jacob went on his journey, and came to the land of the children of the east. . . ." (*vv.* 1–7).

The true worship of God can only be maintained when the passing moments are seen as occurring in God's order. If you try to forecast the way God will work you will get into a muddle; live the life of a child and you will find that every haphazard occasion fits into God's order. 'The cult of the passing moment' means that you resolutely believe that "all things work together for good to them that love God, to them who are the called according to His purpose." Don't be your own god in these matters; be concentrated, not on the haphazard, but on God, who comes to you through the haphazard. Jacob is realizing God's order in the midst of the haphazard circumstances in which he finds himself; in the coming of Rachel he suddenly meets God.

(2) GOD AND THE CULT OF THE PASSIONATE MOMENT (vv. 8–14)

"And Jacob kissed Rachel, and lifted up his voice, and wept" (v. 10).

There is no safer guide in the matter of human love than the Bible, particularly the Old Testament. Solomon says a penetrating thing—"I adjure you, ... that ye stir not up, nor awaken love, until it please"—before the time (The Song of Songs ii. 7), and woe be to any such awakener. Many a man has awakened love before the time, and has reaped hell into the bargain. Love is awakened before the time whenever a man or woman ignores the worship of God and becomes a mere creature of impulsive passions. God cannot guard the natural heart that does not worship Him, it is at the mercy of every vagrant passion stirred by the nearness of another. Unless you are guarded by God in your human relationships you will get a multitude of haphazard affairs that God is not in; there are the same haphazard affairs in the life of a child of God, but God is in them.

Beware of not worshipping God in your emotional history. Watch your fancies and your friends, heed who you love and who loves you, and you will be saved from many a pitfall.

44

(3) GOD AND THE CULT OF THE PARENTHETIC MOMENT
   (*vv.* 15–20)

"And Jacob loved Rachel; and he said, I will serve thee
seven years for Rachel" (*v.* 18).

Jacob was what he was—mean, yet in the most
mixed human life there may come a parenthesis which
is pure and unsullied. Mark well the parentheses God
puts into your human life. There is not a passage in
the whole of the Bible to equal verse 20 for a descrip-
tion of pure human love: "And Jacob served seven
years for Rachel, and they seemed unto him but a few
days, for the love he had to her." Sacrifice for love is
never conscious; sacrifice for duty always has margins
of distress. The nature of love is to give, not to
receive. Talk to a lover about giving up anything, and
he doesn't begin to understand you!

Love is not blind; love sees a great deal more than
the actual, it sees the ideal in the actual, consequently
the actual is transfigured by the ideal. That is a
different thing from 'halo-slinging', which means you
have your own idea about other people and expect
them to live up to it, and then when they don't, you
blame them. An ideal is not a halo, it is reality made
clear to you by intuition. If you love someone you are
not blind to his defects but you see the ideal which
exactly fits that one. God sees all our crudities and
defects, but He also sees the ideal for us; He sees
"every man perfect in Christ Jesus", consequently He
is infinitely patient.

(4) GOD AND THE CULT OF THE PARALLELED MEASURE
   (*vv.* 25–30)

"What is this thou hast done unto me? did not I serve with
thee for Rachel? wherefore then hast thou beguiled me?"
(*v.* 25).

The humour of God is sometimes tragic; He engineers across our path the kind of people who exhibit to us our own characteristics—not very flattering, is it? In this chapter we see the beguiler beguiled; Jacob was deceived, but he also was a deceiver. We say, 'I wonder why this should happen to me?' Remember the Apostle Paul's words: "For he that doeth wrong shall receive again for the wrong ("receive again the wrong" R.V. marg.) that he hath done: and there is no respect of persons" (Colossians iii. 25).

DEGENERATION

Chapters xxix–xxx

Degeneration and backsliding are by no means one
and the same. Degeneration begins in almost imper-
ceptible ways; backsliding in the Scriptural use of the
term is a distinct forsaking of what I know of God and
a deliberate substitution of something other (cf.
Jeremiah ii. 13).

A point on which we need to be alert is that the
presence of the life of the Son of God in us does not
alter our human nature; God does remove the disposition of sin, but He demands of us that our human
nature 'puts on the new man', and no longer fashions
itself according to its former natural desires. This is
what the Apostle Paul means by his use of the term
'mortify' (Colossians iii. 5), viz., destroy by neglect.
The spiritual application is that the natural must be
sacrificed in order that it may be turned into the
spiritual. This law works all through. Esau stands for
the natural life refusing to obey. If I maintain my
right to my natural self I will begin to degenerate and
get out of God's purpose. What happens in my personal life when I am born from above is that the Son
of God is born in me, then comes in this law of the
sacrifice of the natural to the spiritual, and the
possibility of degeneration. If I refuse to sacrifice
the natural, the God-life in me is killed.

(1) WHEN THE REWARD OF SIN IS MORE SINFULNESS

Chapter xxix records the retribution Jacob experienced for his own deceitfulness—Jacob impersonates Esau; Laban makes Leah impersonate Rachel. Beware what you permit in your relationships because you will 'be-done-by-as-you-did', and the reason for it is God. The inexorable law is stated in Matthew vii—"For with what judgment ye judge, ye shall be judged: and with what measure ye mete, it shall be measured to you again." The wrong began with Abraham and Hagar, and it works straight through 'the maddening maze of things'; the only line of extrication is through the Redemption. It is one thing to deceive other people, but you have to get up very early if you want to take in God!

(2) WHERE THE RUIN OF SANCTITY IS MIXED SANCTITY (ch. xxx. 1–24)

Jacob's home becomes a place of friction—no man ever gave his heart to two women—yet gleams of joy come to it, every child is regarded by the Hebrew as a gift of God, and the naming of Jacob's children reveals how closely men felt God to be bound up with their history.

If you indulge in practices which the Holy Spirit condemns, or in imaginations you have no business to indulge in, the appalling lash of ruined sanctity is that 'my sin finds *me* out'. 'If I could only fling the whole thing overboard!'—but you cannot. God has made the way of transgressors hell on earth. The first mark of degeneration is to deem a wrong state permissible, and then propose it as a condition of sanctity. We only turn in disgust from the details in God's Book when we forget who we are. Nothing has ever been done by human nature that any member of the human family may not be trapped into doing; the only safeguard is to keep in the light as God is in the light.

(3) WHERE RETRIBUTION OF SELFISHNESS TURNS TO SPITE (*vv.* 25–43)

Jacob has been robbed, and now he retaliates; his aim is to enrich himself at Laban's expense and he succeeds absolutely—"And the man increased exceedingly, and had large flocks, and maidservants and menservants, and camels and asses" (*v.* 43).

Beware of the inspiration that springs from impulse, because impulse enthrones self-lordship as God. My impulses can never be disciplined by anyone saving myself, not even by God. If my impulses are domineered over by somebody else, that one will find sooner or later that he or she has sat on a safety valve— always a risky thing to do. Unless I discipline my impulses they will ruin me, no matter how generous they may be. The revelation to ourselves in studying other people's lives ought to make us eager to realize that 'in me dwelleth no good thing'.

THE CRISIS IN CIRCUMSTANCES

Chapter xxxi

"And the Lord said unto Jacob, Return to the land of thy fathers" (v. 3).

No man's destiny is made for him, each man makes his own. Fatalism is the deification of moral cowardice which arises from a refusal to accept the responsibility for choosing either of the two destined ends for the human race—salvation or damnation. The power of individual choice is the secret of human responsibility. I can choose which line I will go on, but I have no power to alter the destination of that line once I have taken it—yet I always have the power to get off one line on to the other.

(1) CONFUSION IN CONSECRATION (vv. 4–10)

Jacob would seem to think that to do things openly when you might do them obscurely is a sign of feeble intelligence; all his outwitting has not taught him wisdom. The apparent piece of humbug which these verses record is not really humbug at all, it is a repetition of what happened in the matter of the birthright, in which Isaac and Rebekah, Jacob and Esau, all did wrong, and yet out of it came the fulfilment of God's purpose. The blunder lies in trying to help God fulfil His own word. God's word will be fulfilled, but if I reach its fulfilment through committing sin, God must crush me in chastisement; the chastisement has no part in His order, it comes in under His permissive will.

50

(2) CALL TO CONSCIENCE (vv. 11–13)

Jacob has brought back to him his dream at Beth-el
when God appeared to him and spoke to him—"I am
the God of Beth-el, where thou anointedst a pillar,
where thou vowedst a vow unto Me; now arise, get
thee out from this land, and return unto the land
of thy nativity." Jacob's character exhibits human
nature as it is better than any other Bible character—
the high mountain peaks and the cesspools, they all
come out. No man is so bad but that he is good enough
to know he is bad. Beware of insisting on attainments
which are impossible to human nature before the
possibilities of the Divine nature have come in—
demanding of human nature that it should be what it
never can be. Jesus Christ died for the *ungodly*, for
the *weak*, for *sinners*; if we put the fruits of the Redemption as the reason for God's forgiveness, we
belittle His salvation. God's call comes, not to human
nature, but to conscience, and when a man obeys
what God reveals to a thoroughly awakened conscience, then begins the possibility in human nature of
the expression of the life of God. To experience conviction of sin is not a cause for misgiving, but an
occasion for understanding the impossible thing God
has done in the Redemption.

(3) CALAMITY IN ESTRANGEMENT (vv. 14–35)

"So he fled with all that he had; . . . " (v. 21).

Jacob's flight and its attendant perplexities is the
best unveiling of the unutterable muddle the most
acute human wisdom can get into, and serves as
another indication of the truth of the revelation that
"A man's goings are of the Lord; how then can man
understand his way?" Crises reveal that we don't

believe this, the only God we worship is our own wits.
All through, a personal crisis ought to serve as an
occasion for revealing the fact that God reigns, as well
as compelling us to know our own character. You
may think yourself to be generous and noble until a
crisis comes, and you suddenly find you are a cad and
a coward; no one else finds it out, but you do. To be
found out by yourself is a terrible thing.

"Now Rachel had taken the teraphim, . . ." (v. 34)
In the centre of the family is Rachel, and she outwits
Laban and Jacob by stealing the household gods.
"And Rachel stole the teraphim that were her
father's." (v. 19). There are only two beings a woman
is not too much for, one is God, the other is the devil.
A mascot is a talisman of some sort the presence of
which is supposed to bring good luck. The persistence
of the superstitious element is one of the most indelible
stains on the character of otherwise good people, and
it abounds in our own day. A re-awakening of super-
stition always follows on the heels of gross materialism
in personal and in national life. When once the
'mascot' tendency is allowed in the temple of the
Holy Ghost, spiritual muddle-headedness is sure to
result. Beware of excusing spiritual muddle-headedness in yourself; if it is not produced by the 'Jacob'
reserve, it is produced by the 'Rachel' wit, and the only
way out of the muddle is to walk in the light.

MAHANAIM

Chapter xxxii

Of all the Bible characters Jacob ever remains the best example of the recipient of God's life and power, simply because of the appalling mixture of the good and the bad, the noble and the ignoble in him. His nobility is never far to seek in the midst of it all. We have the notion that it is only when we are pure and holy that God will appear to us; that God's blessing is a sign that we are right with Him. Neither notion is true. Our Lord took care to say that 'God makes His sun to rise on the evil and on the good, and sends His rain on the just and on the unjust'. God's blessings are not to be taken as an indication of the integrity of the character blessed, yet on the other hand the discernment of God's character is determined entirely by the individual character of the person estimating God. "With the merciful Thou wilt shew Thyself merciful;" (Psalm xviii. 24–26). The way I will discern God's character is determined by my own character. God remains true to His character, and as I grow in integrity I discern Him. Jacob's undeservedness, and the fact that God continually blesses him, are brought out very clearly all through his life.

(1) THE VENTURE OF THE MISGIVING WAY

"And Jacob went on his way",

A sense of personal unworthiness is frequently the reaction of overweening conceit; genuine unworthiness

has no conscious interest in itself. A genuinely un-
worthy nature is always possessed of sufficient nobility
to face the inevitable—"And Jacob went on his way,"
that is the noble streak. The study of Jacob under the
light of the Spirit of God is not exhilarating, but it is a
wholesome cure for spiritual swagger. Whenever you
get a real dose of your own unworthiness you are never
conscious of it because you are so certain you are un-
worthy that you have the courage of despair. The first
thing the Spirit of God does when He comes in is to
bring this sense of unworthiness. Most of us suspend
judgment about ourselves, we find reasons for not
accusing ourselves entirely, consequently when we
find anything so definite and intense as the Bible
revelation we are apt to say it exaggerates, until we
are smitten with the knowledge of what we are like in
God's sight. If you can come to God without a feeling
of your own contemptibility it is questionable whether
you have ever come. The most humiliating thing in
self-examination is that the passion of indignation we
indulge in regarding others is the measure of our self-
detection (*see* Romans ii. 1).

(2) THE VISION OF THE MINISTERING WITNESSES

"and the angels of God met him" (*v.* 1).

Isn't that indiscreet of God! The appearances of
God are not so much a testimony to the goodness of
the individual as the revelation of God Himself. Every
estimate of God must be brought to the standard of
the revelation made of Him by our Lord. The appear-
ance of the angels of God is apt to be looked upon
as the result of disordered nerves, but it is only when
external conditions are hopeless to the human outlook
that we are in a fit state to perceive the revelation.

54

We are content where we are as long as things have not got to the hopeless condition, and when we do get there we are sentimentally interested in our own pathos—'Whatever shall I do when this, or that, happens?' When it does happen, you will see the angels of God. There is no such thing as dull despair anywhere in the Bible, there is tragedy of the most appalling order, but an equally amazing hopefulness —always a door deeper down than hell which opens into heaven.

(3) THE VOICE OF THE MASTERING WONDER

"And Jacob said when he saw them, This is God's host: and he called the name of that place Mahanaim" (v. 2).

The sight of the two hosts, the earthly and the heavenly, is a fitting revelation of God's rule and government in this order of things. The reason so few of us see the hosts of God is that we have never let go of things as they are, never let go of our small parochial notions, of the sense of our own whiteness and respectability, consequently there is no room for God at all. Beware of the abortion of God's grace which prostitutes the Holy Spirit to the personal private use of my own whiteness, instead of allowing God by His majestic grace to keep me loyal to His character in spite of everything that transpires. Faith in God does not mean that He presents me as a museum specimen, but it does mean that however ignoble I may feel, I remain true to God's character no matter what perplexities may rage.

God's angelic hosts are like His visible mercies, countless. We are economically drunk nowadays, everybody is an economist, consequently we imagine that God is economical. Think of God in Creation! Think of the number of trees and blades of grass and flowers, the extravagant wealth of beauty no one ever sees! Think of the sunrises and sunsets we never look at! God is lavish in every degree. For God's sake, don't be economical, be God's child.

MISGIVING

Chapter xxxii. 3–21

Misgiving is the pathetic poem of the whole of
human life in a word; it signifies the destruction of
confidence. Many things will destroy confidence; as
in the case of Jacob, cunning and sin will do it, or
cowardice; but in every experience of misgiving there
is an element which it is difficult to define, and the
shallow element is the most difficult. 'I can't understand why I have no confidence in God'; the reason
may be a matter of digestion, not enough fresh air,
or sleep, too much tea—something slight. It is the
shallow things that put us wrong much more quickly
than the big things. The great object of the enemy of
our souls is to make us fling away our confidence in
God; to do this is nothing less than spiritual suicide.
When we experience misgiving because we have sinned
there is never any ambiguity as to its cause, the Holy
Spirit brings conviction home like a lightning flash.

(1) THE APPOINTMENT OF THE MESSENGERS (*vv.* 3–5)

"And Jacob sent messengers before him to Esau his brother
. . ." (*v.* 3).

Jacob has had a vision of God's power, but now he
begins to put prudent methods on foot in case God
should be obliged to let him down on account of his
cunning. We have all got 'Uriah Heep' tucked away
somewhere, his original form is found in Jacob. Every
one of us has the possibility of every type of meanness
57

any human being has ever exhibited; not to believe this is to live in a fool's paradise.

(2) THE APPREHENSION OF THE MANŒUVRES (vv. 6–8)

"And Jacob was greatly afraid and was distressed:" (v. 7).

Jacob has still no intention of confessing his wrong, and his apprehensiveness on this account leads him to manœuvre. Beware of the 'yes-but', of putting your prudence-crutch under the purpose of God when you find His engineering of things has nearly unearthed your own little bag of tricks. Whenever you debate with a promise of God, watch how you begin to manœuvre by your own prudence—but you can't sleep at night. Whenever you manœuvre it keeps up a ferment because it indicates a determination not to confess where you know you are wrong, and when we experience misgiving on account of wrong-doing which we do not intend to confess we are always inclined to put a crutch under God's promise—'Now I see how I can make atonement for my wrong-doing'. Nothing can act as an atonement for wrong saving an absolutely clean confession to God. To walk in the light with nothing folded up is our conscientious part, then God will do the rest.

(3) THE APPEAL OF MISGIVING (vv. 9–12)

"Deliver me I pray Thee, from the hand of my brother, from the hand of Esau: for I fear him . . ." (v. 11).

Prayer in distress dredges the soul (cf. Psalm cvii). It is a good thing to keep a note of the things you prayed about when you were in distress. We remain ignorant of ourselves because we do not keep a spiritual autobiography. Jacob's misgivings while in the attitude of prayer arise from the fact that while there is that in him which causes him to obey God, he is apprehensive lest God should punish him for his wrong-doing; he has to come to the place where he willingly confesses his guilt before God. Remember. Jacob did not turn back; he was cunning and crafty, but he was not a coward. There was not a strand of the physical coward in Jacob, but he was a moral coward by reason of his guilty conscience. His misgivings arose from his misdeeds.

Beware of having plans in your petitions before God; they are the most fruitful source of misgiving. If you pray along the line of your plans misgivings are sure to come, and if the misgivings are not heeded you will pervert God's purpose in the very thing which was begun at His bidding. God begins a work by the inspiration of the Holy Spirit for His own ends entirely and we get caught up into His purpose for that thing, then we begin to introduce our own plans—'I want *this* to produce *that*,' and we storm the throne of God along that line; and the first thing God does is *not* to do it, and we say, 'That must be the devil'. Beware of making God an item, even the principal item, in your programme. God's ways are curiously abrupt with programmes, He seems to delight in breaking them up.

(4) The Atonement for Misdeeds (*vv*. 13–21)

"And he lodged there that night; and took of that which he had with him a present for Esau his brother;" (*v*. 13).

Watch your motive for giving presents; it is a good way of discerning what a mean sneak you are capable of being. The giving of presents is one of the touchstones of character. If your relationship with God is not right in your present-giving, you will find there is an abomination of self-interest in it somewhere, even though you do it out of a warm-hearted impulse; there is a serpent-insinuation in it. It creeps into all our charity unless the life is right with God.

The cunning way in which the present is made to Esau is obvious, and yet Jacob is getting near the place where 'Peniel' is possible. Restitution in some form or other is as certain as that God is on His throne. Restitution on the human plane is the evidence that it was God who designed human nature. Watch the almost uncanny accuracy with which the Holy Spirit will bring a thing back—"Therefore if thou bring thy gift to the altar, and there thou rememberest," the Spirit of God brings it to you direct, ". . . go thy way; first be reconciled to thy brother." Beware how you deal with yourself when God is educating you down to the scruple; it is nearly always some ridiculously small thing that keeps you from getting through to God. Human nature looks for something big, yet it is some little thing, but behind it is the disposition of my prideful right to myself. "First go . . ."

PENIEL

Chapter xxxii. 22–32

Peniel means "face of God", and the word to Moses stands—"And He said, Thou shalt not see My face: for no man shall see Me and live" (Exodus xxxiii. 20). This gives peculiar force to Jacob's words, "I have seen God face to face, and my life is preserved", for Jacob did see God face to face, and he did die, so profound a death that God gave him a new name. "Thy name shall no more be called Jacob, but Israel." That is always the test of the reality of sanctification, not so much that I have received something, but that I have ceased to be my old self. Through disillusionment and shattering Jacob comes out on God's side with a changed name; we drag the purpose of God through our own plans and change His name. We have to learn to distinguish between the impression made on us by a vision, and identification with the One who gave us the vision. The love of God and His forgiveness are the first things we experience, we are not prepared as yet to recognize His other attributes of holiness and justice because that will mean death to everything that does not partake of God's nature.

(1) THE STRUGGLE OF ANGUISH

"And Jacob was left alone;" (v. 24).

This phrase is significant because in his loneliness Jacob goes through the decisive struggle of his life.

We are dealing in this chapter with Jacob the giant, not with the mean man. ". . . and there wrestled a man with him until the breaking of the day." Jacob tried to strangle the answer to his own prayer; his wrestling represents the human fighting with God. The nobler ones in God's sight are those who do not struggle but go through without demur. Abraham did not wrestle, neither did Isaac; Jacob struggles for everything. If a man has difficulty in getting through to God we are apt to imagine it is an indication of a fine character, whereas the opposite is true; he is refusing to yield and is kicking, and the only thing God can do is to cripple him. The characteristics exhibited by Jacob are those of Peter before Pentecost, of Saul of Tarsus before his conversion, a mixture of the dastardly and the heroic, the mean and the noble, all jumbled up. Jacob's wrestling is a profounder thing than the meeting with his brother, there is not one word about Esau in all that follows. Jacob is face to face with his need to acknowledge God and be blessed by Him.

(2) THE SURRENDER OF ALL

"I will not let thee go, except thou bless me" (v. 26).

This is the picture of Jacob's full renunciation. When the supreme crisis is reached in a mixed soul like Jacob something must die, either self-realization or God. To the simpler nature the crisis need not come at all, but to the mean, the ambitious, and the proud, it must come, and God does not show Himself as gentleness, but as adamant. It means death without the slightest hope of resurrection. What it is that goes to death depends on me. Am I willing to let the wrong in me that cannot dwell with God go to death, or willing to let the life of God die out in me? The crisis may be reached in an apparently placid commonplace life, there may be no external sign of it, but there is an internal crumbling away from all that is pure and holy. Jacob was not like that, he did not refuse to go through the inward struggle of his own nature against the blazing holiness of God.

(3) THE SOLICITATION OF APPEAL

"And he said unto him, What is thy name? And he said, Jacob" (v. 27).

The confession has to be made: That is my name—supplanter; sneak; there is no palliation. Jacob had to get to the place where he willingly confesses before God the whole guilt of usurping the birthright. This is full and profound and agonizing repentance. "And he said, Thy name shall be called no more Jacob, but Israel: for thou hast striven with God and with men, and hast prevailed." The warrior of God is not the man of muscle and a strong jaw, but the man of unutterable weakness, the man who knows he has not any power; Jacob is no longer strong in himself, he is strong only in God, his life is no longer marked by striving, but by reliance on God. You cannot imitate reliance on God.

> Not by wrestling, but by clinging
> Shall we be most blest;
>
> . . . . . .
>
> Unconditional surrender
> Brings us God's own peace.

Jacob's wrestling means that he did not want to go through the way he knew he must, he had to come to the end of the best of his natural self, and he struggled in order not to. Then he came to the place where his wisdom was crippled for ever; "and he halted upon his thigh." The symbol is expressive of what it looks

63

like in the eyes of shrewd wordly wisdom to cast your-self unperplexed on God. When we cling to God we learn to kneel for the first time.

If you have never been to 'Peniel' you are sure to come across things that will put your human wisdom into a panic; if you have seen God face to face your circumstances will never arouse any panic in you. We run off at a tangent—anywhere but Peniel, where we would see God "face to face."

THE STILL SMALL VOICE

Chapters xxxiii–xxxv

On the surface everything seemed right enough to Jacob in Shechem, but underneath the surface everything was wrong. Everything is always wrong when the children of God dwell in Shechem instead of at Beth-el. This chapter is the unveiling by God of the actuality of sin.

"And Jacob came in peace to the city of Shechem" (v. 18). One day the hollow 'Shechem' peace was shaken by earthquake—Dinah's fall, and her brothers' crime, rudely awakened Jacob; then God's voice was heard: "Arise, go up to Beth-el, and dwell there."

To enter into peace for ourselves without becoming either tolerantly un-watchful of other lives or an amateur providence over them, is supremely difficult. God holds us responsible for two things in connection with the lives He brings around us in the apparent haphazard of His providence, viz., insistent waiting on God for them, and inspired instruction and warning from God to them. The thing that astonishes us when we get through to God is the way God holds us responsible for other lives.

(1) THE AWAKENING VOICE OF GOD

"And God said unto Jacob, Arise, go up to Beth-el, and dwell there: . . ." (ch. xxxv. 1).

This must be the voice of God; no human voice would ever have said what these words imply. Think what Beth-el meant to Jacob in memory—Beth-el was

65

the geographical place of God to him: "How dreadful
is this place! this is none other but the house of God,
and this is the gate of heaven." Beth-el was the place
where the Divine promises had been given, and vows
made, not yet fulfilled. To go back to Beth-el meant
to acknowledge error. The voice of God to an
awakened soul, when it has heard the voice before, is
never to go forward, but to go back. When the blood
runs high and impulse worships at the shrine of the
heroic, and the nerves strain for the actual doing of
something, we not only do not hear God's voice, we
don't want to hear it. Then when events have produced an earthquake in the personal life, we find that
God was not in the earthquake, but in the still small
voice, 'Go to Beth-el, and stay there'.

(2) THE AROUSING VIRTUE OF GOD (vv. 2–4)

"Then Jacob said unto his household, and to all that were
with him, Put away the strange gods that are among you,
. . ." (v. 2).

Now that Jacob has heard the voice of God speaking
to him he is not afraid to assert his authority in his
household. When you come across a man or woman
who talks to you from God, you know it by the intuition of your spirit and you obey him, scarcely
realizing what you are doing; on looking back you
become aware that it was not a human voice at all
but the voice of God. Simulated authority should be
laughed at, and it is a downright sensible human duty
to do so, but when the authority of God comes to you
through anyone, to rebel against it would be to rebel
against God. But beware of trying to be consistent to
the authority that God gives you over any life on a
particular occasion; you know that God used you then
in that life and you say, 'Now I am always going to

66

have this authority'—that is wrong. Authority never comes from you, but from God through you, therefore let God introduce or withhold as He chooses.

(3) THE APPRECIATED VALUE OF GOD

"And let us arise, and go up to Beth-el; and I will make there an altar unto God, . . ." (*v. 3*).

Every expansion of heart or brain or spirit must be paid for in added concentration. In the meeting with Esau and the marvellous experience of reconciliation with him, Jacob had an expansion of heart, but he did not pay for it afterwards in concentration; he lived loosely in the exalted peace of the expanded life, and suddenly a terrible tragedy breaks up the whole thing. In our personal lives every expansion of heart, whether it is the awakening of human love, or bereavement, must be paid for by watchfulness; if it is not, looseness, the feeling of all-abroadness, ending in moral collapse, is sure to result. It is because people do not understand the way they are made that all the havoc is produced in the lives of those who really have had times with God and experienced expansions of heart, but they have forgotten to concentrate, and the general feeling of looseness is a sure sign that God's presence has gone.

"who answered me in the day of my distress, and was with me in the way which I went"—the implication is, 'when God answered me and brought deliverance, I forgot all about Him'. Jacob settled down in the peace of Shechem, Dinah went to hell, and her brothers to the devil; then God spoke to Jacob. If you allow your mind to be expanded and forget to concentrate on God, the thing that happened in Jacob's domestic life on the big scale will happen in your bodily life on the narrow scale. The vision of what God wants must be paid for by concentration on your part, if it is not, you begin to get all abroad, and in come the 'little foxes', in comes inordinate affection, in come a hundred and one things that were never there before, and down you go. It is not that these things may happen, they *will* happen as sure as God is God, unless you watch and pray, that is, concentrate until you are confirmed in the ways of God.

Innocence must be transfigured into virtue by moral choices. We are all apt to be taken in by a frank nature. The man we call frank says of a wrong thing, 'I'm sorry I did it', and promptly does it again, and we forgive him, while all the time the deepest devilry goes on. The frank nature brings the glamour of virtue without its reality and stings innocence to death. Innocence is not purity, innocence is right for a child, but criminal for a man or woman. Men and women have no business to be innocent, they ought to be virtuous and pure. Character must be attained.

Individuality, impulse, and innocence are the husk of personal life. Individuality, if it goes beyond a certain point, becomes pig-headedness, determined independence. I have to be prepared to give up my independent right to myself in order that my personality may emerge. Impulse is a subtle snare, always and every time; it may start right, but it is a short-cut to fame or infamy, and it is along the line of impulse that lust and temptation comes. Hold back the impulse and you discipline it into character, and it becomes something altogether different, viz., intuition. The same thing with innocence; innocence must be transformed into purity by a series of moral choices. There is no virtue that has not gone through a moral choice. A great many of us make virtues out of necessity.

THE BOY OF GOD

Chapters xxxvii–l

(1) IDEALS OF SEVENTEEN

"Joseph, being seventeen years old, ..." (ch. xxxvii. 2).

The Bible always incarnates ideals in great personalities, and Joseph stands for the magnificent integrity of boyhood; no man thinks so clearly or has such high ideals as in his teens, but unless our ideals find us living in accordance with them they become a mockery. The Bible pays no attention to intellectual and emotional conceptions, but only to the actual manifestation of the ideal. A man may have remarkable conceptions, fine intellectual views, noble ideals and his actual life be beneath contempt, proving that all the high ideals and intellectual conceptions in the world have not the slightest power to bring the life into contact with Reality. There is no room whatever in our Lord's teaching for ideals and a stumbling walk of the feet; there must be an at-one-ment between the God-inspired conceptions and actual life, and the only way this can be brought about is by 'Coming to Me'.

Joseph was amazingly susceptible to God, and he 'dreamed dreams' (see vv. 5, 9). The dreams of the Old Testament are the touch of God on the spirit of a man; always reverence such dreams. "And they hated him the more for his dreams, and for his words" (v. 8). The hatred produced by a sense of superiority in another is the most venomous. This gives the inner meaning of our Lord's words: 'They hated Me without a cause." Beware what you brood on in secret for the fateful opportunity will come when God and the devil will meet in your soul, and you will do according to your brooding, swept beyond all your control. This is a law as sure as God is God. The fateful opportunity came to the brethren who hated Joseph—"And when they saw him afar off, even before he came near unto them, they conspired against him to slay him." Beware of saying, 'Oh well, it doesn't matter much what I think about in secret'; it does, for the opportunity will come when what you think about in secret will find expression and spurt out in an act. The Bible always speaks of sin as it appears in its final analysis. Jesus does not say, 'You must not covet because it will lead to stealing'; He says, 'You must not covet because it *is* stealing'. He does not say, 'You must not be angry with your brother because it will lead to murder'; He says, 'You must not be angry with your brother because it *is* murder'. "Whosoever hateth his brother is a murderer" (1 John iii. 15). When the climax of these things is reached we begin to see the meaning of Calvary.

(2) "His Strength was as the Strength of Ten"

"And the Lord was with Joseph, and he was a prosperous man; and he was in the house of his master the Egyptian" (ch. xxxix. 2).

A life with presence, i.e., an uncommon spirit, redeems any situation from the commonplace. It may be cleaning boots, doing house work, walking in the street, any ordinary thing at all, but immediately it is touched by a man or woman with presence it ceases to be commonplace. The rarest asset to a godly life is to be practically conscientious in every situation. "But the Lord was with Joseph, . . . and gave him favour

70

in the sight of the keeper of the prison" (*v.* 21).
Joseph's adaptability was superb. Adaptability is not
tact—tact is frequently nothing but the moral counter-
part of hypocrisy. Adaptability is the power to make a
suitable environment for oneself out of any set of
circumstances. Most of us are all right if we can live
in our own particular setting, with our own crowd,
but when we get pitchforked somewhere else either we
cannot adapt ourselves, or we adapt ourselves too
easily and lose God. Joseph did not lose God; God was
with Joseph in Egypt as in Canaan; with him in the
prison as in the house of his master. If I simply delight
in a godly atmosphere and refuse to appropriate God
for myself, when I have to leave the godly atmosphere
I will find myself God-less; then my natural adaptability becomes the adaptability to degenerate.

(3) "COMPLETE STEEL"

". . . How then can I do this great wickedness, and sin
against God?" (ch. xxxix. 9).

The phrase 'complete steel' is Milton's definition of
chastity, and is peculiarly appropriate to Joseph.
Personal chastity is an impregnable barrier against evil.
Like virtue, chastity is not a gift, but an attainment
of determined integrity. Unsoiledness may be nothing
more than necessity, the result of a shielded life, and
is no more chastity than innocence is purity. Virtue
and chastity are forged by me, not by God. You can't
drown a cork, and you can't defile Joseph.

Four time over in this chapter is the statement
made, "the Lord was with Joseph." It is the presence
of God that is the secret of victory always. The fear
of the Lord creates an atmosphere in which impure
thoughts and unholy desires die a natural death. "But
so did not I, because of the fear of God" (*see* Nehemiah

v. 15). Joseph knew that the God whom he worshipped was 'of purer eyes than to behold evil, and could not look on iniquity'. The outstanding value of the Bible is that it makes shameful things appear shameful because it never analyses them.

The discovery of the desperate recesses in the human heart is the greatest evidence of the need for the Redemption. The experiences of life awaken possibilities of evil that make you shudder, and as long as we remain under the refuge of innocence we are fools. The appalling things revealed in human lives confirm the words of the great Master of the human heart. Our Lord did not say, *'into the heart of man "these things" are injected'*, but, *"from within, out of the heart of man, proceed . . ."* and then follows the terrible catalogue. We ought to get into the habit of estimating ourselves by this rugged standard. The important thing to remember is that we are better trusting the revelations of Jesus Christ than our own innocence. The only thing that safeguards is the Redemption.

"And God sent me before you to preserve you a remnant in the earth, and to save you alive by a great deliverance" (ch. xlv. 7).

That was Joseph's high vocation, to preserve life. God brings His purposes to pass in spite of all men may do, and often through what they do, and He will utilize the very things which look as if they were going dead against their fulfilment; God goes steadily on and involves us in the fulfilment.

"So now it was not you that brought me hither, but God" (ch. xlv. 8).

"But as for you, ye meant evil against me; but God meant it unto good" (ch. l. 21).